D1547335

THE FIFTY-SIX WHO SIGNED

ST. MARY'S COLLEGE OF MARYLAND LIBRARY
ST. MARY'S CITY, MARYLAND

059571

THE FIFTY-SIX WHO SIGNED

by Sam Fink

The McCall Publishing Company • New York

THE FIFTY-SIX WHO SIGNED
Copyright © 1971 by Sam Fink
All rights reserved.

Published simultaneously in Canada by
Doubleday Canada Ltd., Toronto.

SBN 8415–2038–0
Library of Congress Catalog Card Number: 70–153185
First Printing
Printed in the United States of America

The McCall Publishing Company
230 Park Avenue
New York, N.Y. 10017

To Adelle and David
and Elizabeth.

THE FIFTY-SIX WHO SIGNED

This was the old State House in Philadelphia.
The year was 1776.
The month was July.
The first day.
In a room with comfortable chairs were the delegates
to the Second Continental Congress. They had convened
to discuss the resolution on independence.
It was hot and humid. Horseflies buzzed and bit, causing
a constant sound of slapping and swatting.
Delegations from each colony felt one another out.
Some were in doubt. South Carolina and Pennsylvania
opposed the resolution. Delaware was split.

Edward Rutledge, South Carolina, sensing the tension, suggested a postponement of the vote until the next day. The motion carried.

Next day the resolution, first introduced by Richard Henry Lee, Virginia, on June 7, was put to a vote. Each group voted in favor except New York, who abstained. Their instructions had not yet arrived.

John Adams thought July 2 ought to be Independence Day. Nobody listened. They had to get on with the actual Declaration.

Back on June 11 a committee had been formed to prepare a Declaration of Independence. Jefferson, one of the committee, was appointed to do the writing.

By June 28 the Declaration was in good enough shape to afford the delegates in Philadelphia an opportunity to read and study it. Suggestions and changes were called for.

The Declaration was presented on the morning of the third. Further corrections, additions, and subtractions were made. Jefferson incorporated these as he worked through the night on his portable desk in the parlor of a furnished apartment at Market and Seventh.

The fourth came up bright and sunny with a fresh wind from the southeast.

The corrected Declaration was read aloud. There were further changes from the floor. From the time Jefferson's first draft was finished, a grand total of eighty-six changes were made.

A vote was called for. Beginning with New Hampshire in the north, and working down to Georgia in the south, the vote was recorded. All voted aye, except New York. The New York delegates personally favored the Declaration. They could not vote because their instructions had not arrived. Affirmative instructions finally arrived on July 15.

There were no cheers. No outburst of applause. That was it. The Declaration of Independence was born, the beginning of the country.

All the men who eventually signed were not present in Philadelphia that day. On August 2, the beautifully designed parchment was ready to be signed. It took months to get all the signatures. The delegates had scattered.

Take a look at all the men. See how they signed their names.

Josiah Bartlett

JOSIAH BARTLETT, often listed first because he represented New Hampshire, which was the first delegation called upon to cast its vote.

His signature is straightforward and sure.

He practiced medicine and was a respected country doctor. Became a colonel in the militia and was appointed Justice of the Peace. Supported the Patriots when it was not the popular thing to do. Because of this he was dismissed as justice of the peace.

When spiteful Tories burned his house and possessions, his finances suffered a severe blow. Because of this he had to decline to serve with the First Continental Congress.

Toward the end of his career he was elected chief executive of New Hampshire.

Couldn't stand long-winded talkers. "Get to the point," he'd often say.

He was forty-six when he signed.

Wm Whipple

WILLIAM WHIPPLE was a merchant from Portsmouth. In his youth he was a sailor. Became master of a ship at twenty-one. Saved his money as he sailed the seven seas and went into business with his brother Joseph before he was thirty.

As the fire for independence got hotter he decided to quit the business and devote his energies to the cause. He was sour on England and the taxes.

He became a very spirited general, commanding New Hampshire troops during the war, one of the few signers who was active in the combat.

So good was he as a general that in New Hampshire he is remembered as General Whipple. Today some people don't even know his first name was William.

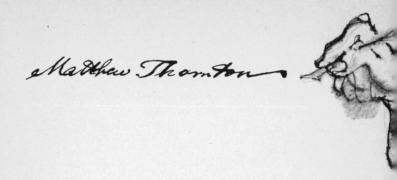

MATTHEW THORNTON was a physician. He was sixty-two, a big man—well over six feet—with black eyes and hair to match.

Born in Ireland to Scottish parents, he came to America when he was four.

A very serious man. You can see it in his signature. Hardly a wasted stroke. Yet it is said that he was an entertaining storyteller.

In 1746 he served as under-surgeon with the New Hampshire troops on the Louisburg expedition. He was then appointed colonel of the militia, a title he held for some years.

He remained active until he died at eighty-nine. Among his papers is the manuscript for an unpublished book, *Paradise Lost: Orthe Origin of the Evil Called Sin.*

His tombstone in Merrimack, New Hampshire, simply says: "An Honest Man."

John Hancock

JOHN HANCOCK was thirty-nine and rich. He inherited a fortune from his uncle, Thomas Hancock, who had raised him from age seven, after his own father had died.

He wore his money well and was quite generous. One of the reasons he opposed British rule was that it hurt his business.

A little flamboyant at times, particularly in his dress, he did put his fortune on the line when he sided with the Patriots. He contributed sums of money as well as his time and energy.

After the war he was elected governor of Massachusetts nine consecutive times.

For the Declaration he signed his name bigger than usual. He wanted to make sure King George III would see it and know exactly where he stood.

Died at fifty-six and was buried in Boston after a week-long, drawn-out funeral ceremony.

Saml Adams

SAMUEL ADAMS was fifty-three. A Harvard man, he lived his entire life in Massachusetts. His grandfather Henry Adams came to America in 1636 from Somerset, England.

Bored with his malthouse, a family business, he turned his attention to public affairs. Did his most effective work behind the scenes. Not what we call a "showboat."

While he chased his dream of independence, his second wife, Elizabeth Wells, struggled with the family finances. Somehow her patience and love kept the household going.

He was a devout, compassionate man. His greatest contributions to the country were made before the Revolution. His star dwindled and dimmed after the war. He had one cause. When it was achieved he could find no other.

He was middle-sized, gray-eyed, and long-nosed. Pleasant, but he could scowl.

It is said he instigated the Boston Tea Party.

Robt Treat Paine

ROBERT TREAT PAINE, forty-five, another Harvard man, was born on Beacon Hill in Boston. Son of a clergyman, his family thought he ought to follow in his father's footsteps. Instead he chose law. Was a member of the First Continental Congress.

Although he was a Patriot, he believed there could be reconciliation with the mother country. He was a questioner, an objection raiser, a doubter. Nevertheless, when the time arrived for independence and revolution, he went along.

He signed his name in one swift move, never lifting his quill.

After the war he helped to draft the state constitution for Massachusetts and was appointed to the state supreme court.

He lived until he was eighty-three.

Elbridge Gerry

ELBRIDGE GERRY, a dapper little man with a dapper little signature.

He was only thirty-two when he signed, yet he was wealthy. His father had built a shipping business at Marblehead, Massachusetts, where Elbridge grew up.

Third of a dozen children, he thought to study medicine at Harvard. Changed his mind and joined his father in business and helped the venture prosper.

He was suspicious, had no sense of humor, and stuttered. A controversial figure, getting in and out of trouble all his life because of his inconsistencies.

His fortune dwindled. He died burdened with debt. The Congress had to pay for his burial.

He was appointed as a member of a mission to France in 1797. His conduct was regarded by some as unwise and questionable. However, President John Adams, who had made the appointment, never questioned his patriotism.

He died in his seventy-first year as vice-president to James Madison.

John Adams

JOHN ADAMS, forty, an impatient man from Massachusetts. One of the prime sparks that helped to ignite the flame of independence. Studied at Harvard and practiced law. A deeply learned man, he was on the dumpy side and got fatter as time passed.

Unlike his cousin Sam, his star rose after the Revolution. He was in the foreign service and was the first vice-president of the United States and second President.

He was devoted to his wife, Abigail. There is much correspondence between them. He always found time to write to her no matter where he was.

Their son, John Quincy Adams, achieved the presidency years later. And there followed a long line of Adamses who made noteworthy marks in government and the world of letters.

STEPHEN HOPKINS, second oldest to sign, at sixty-nine, was a Providence, Rhode Islander. A self-taught man through lots of reading, he entered public life when he was twenty-five.

A man of modest means, his long, practical experience brought balance to the Congress. He had been a surveyor, a farmer, a merchant. He had served as chief justice of Rhode Island and had been elected governor nine times. A patriot to the bone, he knew the high cost of liberty. For him war was the only way.

Though not an excessive drinker, it was bandied about that when he had a few he liked to stay up all night and talk. Just so long as he had company.

His signature wobbles, scratches, and stutters. He suffered from palsy and writing was very difficult. He lived to see the end of the war, his country freed, and peace. He died in his seventy-ninth year.

William Ellery

WILLIAM ELLERY, a ready wit, a prolific letter writer, a Harvard-educated lawyer, well-read, often entertained himself by writing epigrams as he sat in meetings.

His great-grandfather arrived in America in the middle of the 1600s. By the time William Ellery came along the family was well established.

His career began as a so-so merchant in Newport. It wasn't until he settled to the practice of law in his early forties that he began to fulfill the promise that was in him.

He was forty-eight when he signed and he lived in Newport, Rhode Island, until he was ninety-two.

In 1790 President Washington appointed him collector of customs for Newport. He held the post for thirty years.

When the Declaration was signed, he stationed himself where he could study the faces of each of the signers. Said he, "All showed undaunted resolution."

Roger Sherman

ROGER SHERMAN started his career as a shoemaker in western Connecticut. He had little education. By reading and studying he learned the law, how to conduct business, and how to write an almanac. He was a book merchant in New Haven and was appointed treasurer of Yale. One of the country's first self-made men.

Little by little he became involved in the public affairs of Connecticut.

His clothes were severly plain, his appearance awkward and stiff. Had a strange habit of grasping the wrist of his left arm with his right hand when he spoke.

He was a prodigious worker. Awakened at five in the morning and went right to work.

He wore his hair very long. Kept his speeches very short. Never said anything foolish.

He was fifty-five when he signed. At seventy he came down with typhoid. Two years later he died while serving as United States senator.

Oliver Wolcott

OLIVER WOLCOTT was forty-nine, distinguished, and a big name in Connecticut. Youngest of a family of fifteen children, he was first in class for four years before graduating from Yale. While his father was governor he was appointed sheriff of Litchfield. As time passed he became more and more interested and involved in public matters. He was a judge and he served in the militia.

He was not present when the Declaration was voted on. Signed the document in October, 1776, in Philadelphia. Some say that it was ill health that kept him from Philadelphia; others believe that he was busy bringing from New York to Litchfield a statue of George III that was to be melted down to make bullets.

An excellent soldier, he served as a general during the war. Elected governor of Connecticut in 1796, he died in office at age seventy-one.

WILLIAM WILLIAMS of Lebanon, Connecticut, substituted for Oliver Wolcott. Resigned a colonel's commission in the militia to go to Philadelphia for the vote.

Son of a minister, graduate of Harvard, he studied theology with his father. Served in the French and Indian War, after which he returned to Lebanon and became interested in the town's affairs.

He backed his patriotism with his purse. Helped write many of the state papers for the governor of Connecticut, Jonathan Trumbull. He met Mary, the governor's daughter, while going over some papers. After a short courtship he married her.

Generally, a quiet man. When he felt something strongly or was upset, he could burst into a rage. His language would turn purple—a dirty purple.

He lived until he was eighty and is buried in Lebanon.

Sam^a Huntington

SAMUEL HUNTINGTON celebrated his birthday on July 3, while the document was being worked over. He turned forty-five. There is no record of anybody saying happy birthday, Sam.

He was the son of a farmer. His first job was as apprentice to a barrel-maker. Had little formal education, was mainly self-taught, and studied law on his own. Practiced and lived in the town of Norwich, Connecticut.

Before the war he was king's attorney. During the war he was chosen president of Congress. Later became chief justice of the Connecticut supreme court and was elected twelve times to the governorship.

He died in office at age sixty-four.

Of some little interest is that he was economical to a fault. Today, he'd be called a tightwad. The word then was parsimonious.

LEWIS MORRIS of New York, born to wealth, an aristocrat to the hilt.

A Yale graduate, he enjoyed the social life of Westchester County in New York. Tall, good-looking, he added to his fortune when he married Mary Walton, a wealthy woman in her own right. With so much to lose it is unusual that he pitched in with the Patriots and the hazards of the revolution.

Member of the first Continental Congress, he took leave in June of 1776, to take command of the Westchester militia.

Not present when the Declaration was voted on, he returned to Philadelphia in September to sign. He was fifty.

After the war he returned to Westchester County and devoted himself to rebuilding his estate. He died at seventy-one.

Phil. Livingston

PHILIP LIVINGSTON was born to great wealth and used it well. Physically, he was huge, very active, a blustery man. Born in Albany, New York, educated at Yale, he was instrumental in the establishment of King's College (Columbia).

Went into the importing business in New York City and increased his fortune. He contributed large sums to help organize a hospital and the New York Society Library.

He was with the army and not in Philadelphia on July 4. Historians question whether he would have signed at that moment. He wanted further discussion and debate. Thought the country could turn to bitter civil war if set free by England. However, he did sign the document in Philadelphia the following month.

Several other members of the Livingston family contributed much to the country in its infancy.

FRANCIS LEWIS, a Welshman who came to New York and made good. Didn't get here until he was twenty-five. He came alone and brought his business experience with him. With hard work and imagination he made a fortune. He was rich enough to retire in his early fifties. British moves threatened his wealth. This drew him into public life.

As part of the New York delegation, he could not vote for the Declaration on July 4. Instructions had not arrived in Philadelphia. He did return to Philadelphia the following month to sign.

A quiet man, not much of a debater.

His house on Long Island was burned by the British during the war and his wife was taken prisoner. His fortune dwindled.

He was sixty-three when he put his name to the parchment and he lived to the nice old age of ninety.

WILLIAM FLOYD was so reserved he seemed cold and aloof. You could see him in a room and never notice him. Perhaps he was shy, as indicated by his scrunched-up signature.

He was born in Brookhaven, Long Island, New York, of Welsh parents; had very little schooling; inherited a large estate at a tender age.

He was a major general in the militia. Though not a debater, he was always found voting with the "zealous friends of liberty" while a member of the first and second Continental Congresses.

The war just about ruined him financially. With what he had left, he picked up and moved to Oneida County in New York, where he finished out his life.

He lived until he was eighty-six.

Jno Witherspoon

JOHN WITHERSPOON was a striking man, medium height, potbelly-stout, and homely. These features made a strong impression. Nobody could overlook his presence.

He was a Scottish clergyman before he came to New Jersey. He headed the College of New Jersey (later Princeton) and put his main effort toward the development of the Presbyterian Church.

Introduced the philosophy of "common sense" to the new world. James Madison, fourth president of the United States, was one of his students.

An excellent speaker, he never lost his Scottish burr. Many of his sermons were in support of the Patriots and independence.

On July 2 in Philadelphia, as the resolution was being debated, he stood up and said, "The country was not only ripe for the measure [independence] but in danger of rotting for the want of it."

Believed the proper use of the English language important in the development of the country.

Fifty-three when he signed. In his last years injuries took his eyesight. He was blind when he died at seventy-one in Princeton.

Rich? Stockton

RICHARD STOCKTON was a prime mover in the development of Princeton, New Jersey.

Sent to Scotland, he convinced Witherspoon to come to New Jersey to head the college from which Stockton had graduated.

A lawyer with a successful practice, he avoided politics. In time, his success and wealth gradually involved him in public affairs.

His public career was brief. He declined a job as chief justice of New Jersey in order to remain in Congress. The war came nearer and the British overran New Jersey. He moved his family to safety; was betrayed and captured. His imprisonment was cruel—wrecked his health. He was returned in a prisoner exchange but by then his health was gone. He was an invalid until he died in 1781 at age fifty.

Signed when he was forty-five. He either used a blunt quill or had too much ink on it.

Fra! Hopkinson

FRANCIS HOPKINSON of New Jersey. At thirty-eight, talented, sensitive, lawyer, author, musician, composer, artist, caricaturist, good companion.

An animated man, always on the go. Busy, busy, constantly bubbling. Even found time to design the Stars and Stripes flag of the country.

He foresaw the Declaration before it was born in an essay entitled "A Prophecy."

An intimate friend of Franklin and a lifelong correspondent of Jefferson and a friend to many more.

All his talents were put to use in the cause of independence.

Lived until he was fifty-three.

John Hart

JOHN HART lived in Hopewell, New Jersey. He was a farmer and owned a grist mill. Neighbors called him "Honest John." Had little schooling but lots of horse sense. With this simple asset and hard work he became a man of importance in his community.

He was elected to the Continental Congress in June and voted for independence in July. He was sixty-five.

During the war his lands and home were laid waste and his mill destroyed. The British were hot on his tail. He had to flee and hide out in the mountains. Age and strain drained his health.

Unfortunately, he died before the war had been won.

ABRAHAM CLARK could raise the hackles of an opponent, though in appearance he seemed so gentle.

Antagonistic.

Born in Elizabeth, New Jersey, with little formal education, he became the poor man's lawyer. It is not known whether he was ever admitted to the bar, but practice he did.

Benjamin Rush said of him: "He's sensible but cynical and quick to see weakness and defects in men and ideas." He could belittle, ridicule, and tear down. Yet no one ever doubted his sincerity and integrity.

Served as sheriff of Essex County and as clerk of the state assembly before being elected to the Second Continental Congress.

He voted against the adoption of the Constitution until it contained the Bill of Rights.

Signed the Declaration at fifty, died at sixty-eight.

Beny. a Franklin

BENJAMIN FRANKLIN was a philosopher, a scientist, a wit, a writer, and the oldest man present. He was seventy.

He was educated in a printing shop.

He followed his own advice from the book he wrote, *Poor Richard's Almanac* and at forty-two was rich enough to turn over the management of his printing shop to another. This allowed him time to pursue anything and everything that aroused his curiosity. Philadelphia was his home. His interests there were as varied as establishing a college (University of Pennsylvania) to flying a kite in a lightning storm.

He spent many years in Europe representing the colony's interests. He returned to America just before the Second Continental Congress and represented Pennsylvania. Though he could understand the British point of view, there was no question where he stood on independence.

After the war he was the first American foreign minister to France. He lived until he was eighty-four.

John Morton

JOHN MORTON was a farmer of Swedish descent.

His stepfather, a man with a good background, educated him at home. As he matured he involved himself with politics and was eventually appointed associate justice of the supreme court of Pennsylvania.

He had thoughtfully made up his mind about independence. Definitely. He was so positive that he was instrumental in persuading other delegates from Pennsylvania to vote for independence.

Some of his friends were dismayed and upset by his position. They felt let down and deserted.

Just before his death in 1777, before independence had been won, his last words to his friends were: "Tell them they will live to see the hour when they shall acknowledge it [swinging Pennsylvania for independence] to have been the most glorious service I ever rendered my country."

James Wilson

JAMES WILSON, a Scotsman, was well-educated when he came to Pennsylvania in his early twenties.

He had studied at St. Andrews, Glasgow, Edinburgh. In Philadelphia he was taught law by John Dickinson.

He was short-sighted and squinted, which made him look stern. He moved to Carlisle, Pennsylvania, and built a good law practice.

An excellent speaker, a good writer, he wrote a pamphlet denying the authority of the British Parliament.

When the war started he turned conservative and lost his popularity. He sided with the rich aristocrats. So unpopular did he become that he was beaten by a mob.

After the war he became active again and was appointed associate justice of the Supreme Court, where he performed well.

Speculation in land was his downfall. He overextended himself. His creditors were parked on his doorstep when he died in Edenton, North Carolina, where he had fled. The year was 1798. He was fifty-five.

Robt Morris

ROBERT MORRIS, financier from Pennsylvania.

Born in Liverpool (a Liverpudlian), came to America when he was thirteen, to Chesapeake Bay, from where his father exported tobacco.

He was taught a minimum and put to work. He was a natural in the business. Caught on fast and was soon made a partner of Willing, Morris & Company. He accumulated lots of money in a hurry.

His fortune did not stop him from siding with the Patriots. Critics said he did so to protect his business interests. John Adams didn't doubt it but considered him honest and useful.

When the Continental Treasury was almost broke, he came to the rescue by raising public funds. He organized the financing of weapons and ammunition.

Unable to shake off controversy, his critics continued to believe he used his position in Congress for personal gain.

In 1798 he lost his fortune by speculating in undeveloped land. He tried to escape from his creditors but was caught and jailed for three years. After his release he lived but another five years and died in obscurity. An ignoble finish to what was once a bright flame.

Geo. Taylor

GEORGE TAYLOR may have been born in Ireland. It isn't known for sure. He was a businessman in Durham, which is in Bucks County, Pennsylvania. He ran an iron furnace.

He opposed British rule as far back as 1763. Served six years in the provincial assembly. Then he became inactive. Passage of the British Coercive Act and the news of the Boston Tea Party rekindled his interest.

Sent to the Second Continental Congress to replace one of the Pennsylvanians who did not care to approve the Declaration. This appointment was on July 20, so he was not in Philadelphia when the vote was taken. However, he did approve the Declaration and was there for the signing in August.

Of him it has been said that he had little stomach for the world of politics. He died in 1781, aged sixty-five.

GEORGE ROSS, the lawyer from Lancaster, Pennsylvania, who knew how to laugh. His father was a Scots clergyman and gave him a fine education.

He studied law in his stepbrother John's office in Philadelphia and practiced there for a short time before moving to Lancaster.

At first he was a staunch Loyalist. Served twelve years as crown prosecutor. By 1776, the tension in the land caused him to switch his sentiments to the cause of the Patriots.

He was a popular man and excellent company. Not only did he know how to laugh and tell a story, he knew how to eat and enjoy it.

In 1779 he suffered a severe attack of the gout and died at age forty-nine. He was not chosen as a delegate to the Second Continental Congress until July 20. However, he was in Philadelphia in August for the actual signing of the Declaration.

Jas. Smith

JAMES SMITH, an Irishman, came to America when he was about ten. Joined his family in Chester County, Pennsylvania. Went to school in Philadelphia, studied law with his brother George, in Lancaster, Pennsylvania, and then went on to build his own successful practice.

An adventurer, he spent five years in Cumberland County, the western frontier, helping to develop the land.

He moved back to York, Pennsylvania, resumed his law practice, and went into the iron business. He organized a militia of York residents and was the colonel in charge.

He had a good sense of humor and was a natural-born storyteller.

The details of his life story went up in smoke when all of his papers accidentally burned.

He was not present on July 4 when the Declaration was voted on because he was elected on July 20. He was in Philadelphia in August for the signing. He signed at fifty-seven and died at eighty-seven.

GEORGE CLYMER of Pennsylvania was orphaned when he was one year old. His Uncle William Coleman, a well-to-do Philadelphia merchant, adopted him, cherished him, and gave him his start in the business world.

He built upon the business his uncle left him and as a prosperous merchant he met George Washington. The two became friends for life.

He was a better writer than he was a speaker. A red-hot Patriot, he exchanged all his English money for new Continental currency before the struggle for independence became a war. He put his money where his heart was.

Thirty-seven when he signed, he continued his activities in public business until he died in 1813.

Signing the Declaration was one of the happiest things he ever did. At the time he said, "This is my dearest wish."

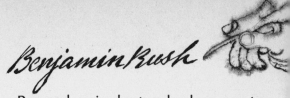

Benjamin Rush

BENJAMIN RUSH, a Pennsylvania doctor, had energy to spare. He had a constant source of this characteristic and it kept him going for sixty-seven years.

He was only thirty when he signed, one of the youngest present.

Born near Philadelphia, he graduated from the College of New Jersey (Princeton), began his study of medicine in Philadelphia, continued it in London and Edinburgh. Practiced medicine and taught at the University of Pennsylvania.

He was full of fire. Jumped into situations without looking. Took sides with no idea of the consequences. Quixotic.

His loose pen got him into difficulty with George Washington. An anonymous letter he wrote to Patrick Henry urged that Washington be replaced as general of the Continental Army. To his embarrassment the letter was uncovered. A dark cloud enveloped his name and ended his military service as surgeon general. In time his enthusiasm and verve helped him to regain his stature.

A prolific writer, he left many papers for historians. A friend of both John Adams and Jefferson, he brought the two together after they had become unfriendly. John Adams appointed him treasurer of the Mint.

He helped fight a yellow fever epidemic in Philadelphia in 1793 by the process of bloodletting. This was sharply criticized by other professionals as no cure or treatment for the disease.

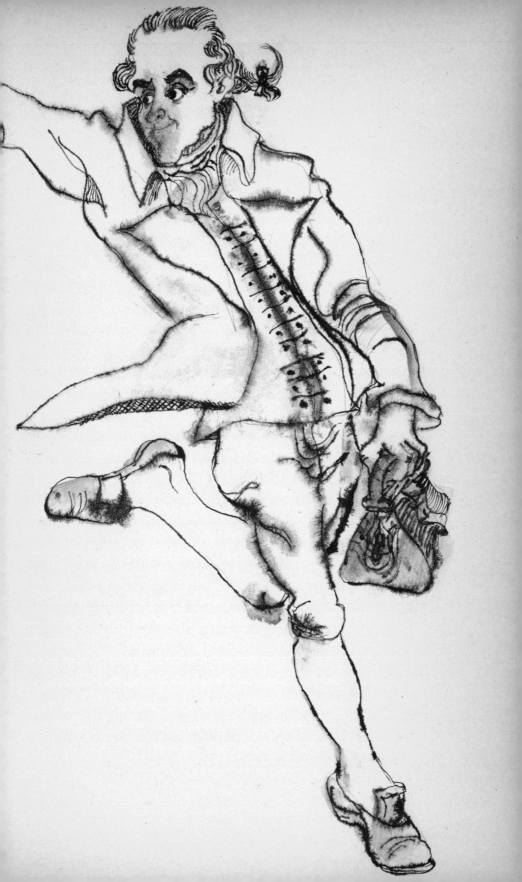

Description by John Adams of CAESAR RODNEY of Delaware:

"Caesar Rodney is the oddest-looking man in the world; he is tall, thin and slender as a reed, pale; his face is not bigger than a large apple, yet there is sense and fire, spirit, wit, and humor in his countenance."

A good portion of his face was cancerous. He paid it no notice. He suffered, looked horrible, and died before his time.

Son of a Delaware planter, he was educated at home. Entered public life early and was active for a dozen years before the big day in 1776.

On June 30, he arrived home after presiding over the June assembly of Delaware. A message from Thomas McKean informed him that a vote for independence would be taken in Philadelphia the following day. McKean was for independence; the other delegate, George Read, was against. Rodney's vote was needed to bring Delaware into line. Dramatically, he rode the night through in a driving rainstorm, arriving in Philadelphia in time to turn the Delaware vote in favor of independence.

He was a general in the militia, president of Delaware during the war. His health declined rapidly after independence was won. A bachelor all his life, he died in 1784, aged fifty-five.

Geo Read

GEORGE READ, tall, thin, and stern, was a little reluctant at first. His fellow delegates, Rodney and McKean, won him over. Convinced him that the time had come for independence. Once he signed, he became a staunch advocate and fighter for the cause.

Born in Maryland, the son of an Irish father and a Welsh mother, he made his home in New Castle, Delaware. He studied law in Philadelphia and practiced there before returning to Delaware to become a member of the House of Assembly. Held that position for twelve years.

After the war he continued to contribute to the growth and development of Delaware and the young nation. In his declining years he resigned from the U. S. Senate to become chief justice of Delaware.

He lived until he was sixty-five.

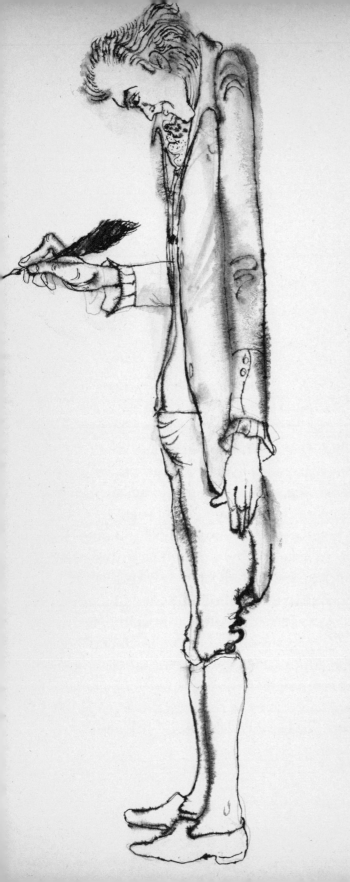

THOMAS MCKEAN, Delaware delegate, was quarrel-some, had little patience, and could get you "mad" at him without half trying. Nonetheless, he was talented and had ability. Tact is what he lacked.

Born in Pennsylvania of Scots-Irish parents, he studied law in Philadelphia. He spread his practice to three states: New Jersey, Pennsylvania, and Delaware. A continental big-time operator, he made lots of money and held on to it. At one time he held office in two states. Eventually he gave most of his time to Pennsylvania.

He was the one who summoned Rodney to come to Philadelphia. As soon as the vote for independence was taken, he left to take his post as colonel with a Pennsylvania military group called the "Associators." He was not around for the signing in August.

The authenticated copy of the Declaration of January 17, 1777, does not carry his signature. It is not known when he signed.

Charles Carroll of Carrollton

CHARLES CARROLL of Carrollton, so called so that he could be distinguished from other Charles Carrolls in the family. His father was Charles Carroll of Annapolis.

Born in Annapolis, Maryland, to great wealth, he became the richest man in America. His estate was worth more than £200,000, making him America's first millionaire.

The only Catholic to sign. He was educated by Jesuits, spent time in Europe, learned to speak French, studied law in Paris and London, finally returned to Maryland when he was twenty-eight.

There were disadvantages in being Catholic. There was prejudice; in Maryland, Catholics couldn't be lawyers, could not teach the young. In 1773 he published a series of articles denouncing government decrees without legislative action. That began his career as a public servant. He was quickly recognized as a staunch Patriot.

After the war he was a member of the U.S. Senate. Resigned to return to the Maryland legislature.

He lived until 1832. Died at the ripe old age of ninety-five, four years after he laid the cornerstone of the Baltimore & Ohio Railroad. He outlived all the other signers.

Wm. Paca

WILLIAM PACA was born to a prosperous family established in Maryland for several generations. Records are not available, but it is said the Pacas originally came from Italy.

Well-educated, he received his master's degree from the College of Philadelphia, studied the law in Annapolis, and completed his legal studies at the Inner Temple in the City of London. He began his legal practice in Annapolis and quickly made his presence felt in the Patriots' cause.

A member of the First as well as the Second Continental Congress, he proved to be a great worker behind the scenes. He achieved the governorship of Maryland and was later appointed U.S. district judge.

Always well-liked and respected, Paca was a quiet man whose talents were greater than his reputation.

He lived until he was fifty-eight.

Samuel Chase

SAMUEL CHASE, Maryland, a big red-faced man, despised by some, loved by others, had a turbulent life.

His father, an Anglican clergyman, educated him in the classics. He studied law in Annapolis and practiced in Baltimore. Immediately upon arriving in Baltimore he became involved in public affairs. As a delegate to the Second Continental Congress — as well as the First — he made a last-minute ride from Baltimore to Philadelphia to arrive in time to vote. His trip may have been more difficult than Caesar Rodney's, but it didn't get the same notice.

During the war, he was caught taking advantage of inside information that allowed him to make a killing in the flour business. His career plummeted. By 1789 he was broke. Turmoil was his partner; nevertheless, he made his way back. President Washington appointed him associate justice of the Supreme Court. His intellect was sharp, his manner atrocious and somewhat partisan. So much so that he was impeached in Jefferson's administration. A trial proved he had not broken any laws; he was acquitted.

He was called "Bacon Face" because he was red, fat, and salty.

Thos. Stone

THOMAS STONE, a quiet man from Maryland, great-great-grandson of a proprietary governor, was born in Charles County. His forebears came to America in the middle of the the 1600s when Lord Baltimore owned the colony and the proprietary governor was his represent-ative.

He studied law in Annapolis and practiced in Fred-erick. Tall, well-proportioned, pleasant, mild-mannered, there is little to be learned of him, for he left few papers or records.

His career was short. In 1787, grieved by his wife's death, he quit work to take a trip to England. Awaiting a vessel in Alexandria, Virginia, he took sick and died.

His home in Charles County, Maryland, was called "Habre-de-Venture." He was buried there at age forty-four.

Richard Henry Lee

RICHARD HENRY LEE, strong of feature, an excellent speaker, introduced the original resolution for independence in Congress on June 7, 1776, at Philadelphia.

Born of a distinguished Virginia family at "Stratford" in Westmoreland County, he was educated in Europe and trained for public service. Elected to the House of Burgesses in his mid-twenties, he joined with Patrick Henry in the fight for independence.

Friendly with the New England Patriots John and Sam Adams, he became the leader of the Virginia Patriots.

After the war he was against the adoption of the Constitution until the Bill of Rights was added. Served as one of Virginia's senators in the U.S. Senate. His health began to decline; he suffered from attacks of gout and resigned his post.

The Lee family played an important role in the early history of Virginia and the development of the country.

He was sixty-two when he died.

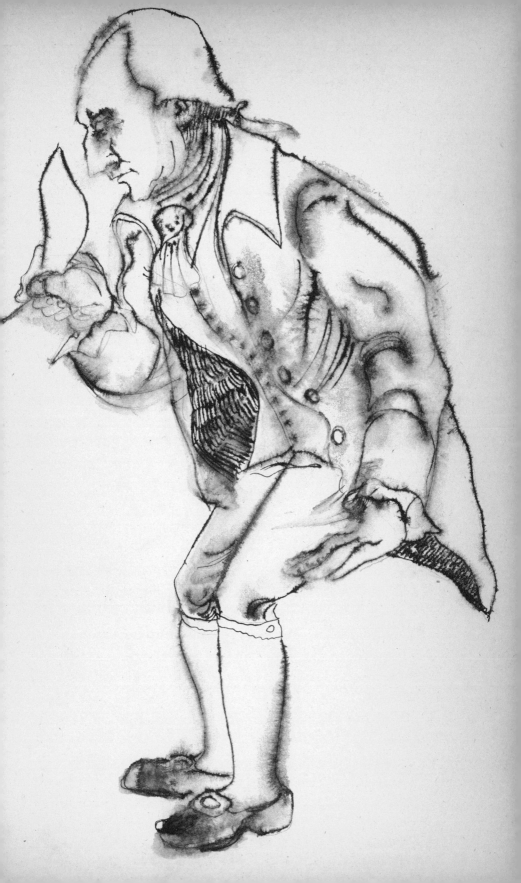

Th Jefferson

THOMAS JEFFERSON of Virginia wrote the Declaration of Independence. He was part of a committee appointed on June 11 to draft a declaration for independence. The committee chose him to do the writing because of his clarity and style. By June 28, after discussions with Franklin and John Adams, the first draft of the Declaration was ready for review by the delegates in Philadelphia.

Born with a silver spoon in his mouth, he inherited a large estate from his father. As if that wasn't enough, he married Mrs. Martha Skelton, a wealthy widow.

He was born in Albemarle County, educated by private tutors, attended the College of William and Mary, where his appetite for science was whetted. Studied law for five years and read just about anything he could put his hands on.

At twenty-six he was elected to the House of Burgesses in Virginia. In 1775 he was sent to Congress as a back-up man for Peyton Randolph, in case Randolph might be needed back home. This was Jefferson's introduction to the big scene and the road that led to the presidency.

Lover of the outdoors, a good farmer, an excellent horseman, he rode until the time of his death.

His work, his ideas, his efforts were powerful forces in the development of the country. Freedom of the individual was his prime concern.

On his tombstone, a simple obelisk he designed, is the inscription he himself wrote:

Here was buried
Thomas Jefferson
author of the Declaration of American Independence
of the Statute of Virginia for religious freedom
and father of the University of Virginia

Benj Harrison

BENJAMIN HARRISON was the fifth in line of men in the distinguished Harrison family to be named Benjamin. To separate himself from the other Benjamins, he referred to himself as Benjamin Harrison "the Signer."

He was a big man, physically, with a hot complexion. Attended the College of William and Mary and was elected to the Virginia House of Burgesses in his early twenties. He served for twenty-five years, often as Speaker. This experience came in handy when he presided over the debates on the resolution for independence.

Although he was a bit more conservative than Patrick Henry, he was a Patriot. Didn't get along too well with the New Englanders; they thought him pompous and stuffy.

One of his seven children, William Henry Harrison, became President of the United States. A great-grandson, Benjamin Harrison, also became President.

He was elected governor of Virginia for several terms. He led an active life until the very end. He suffered from the gout and died at sixty-five.

George Wythe

GEORGE WYTHE (pronounced like Smith), a quiet man with a good mind, lacked the fire of leadership.

He was born on a Virginia plantation, and his father died when he was a child. An older brother received the inheritance, leaving him out in the cold. His warm Quaker mother was his teacher. So good was the start she gave him that he was able to master Latin and Greek on his own. All through life his speeches and writings were sprinkled with Latin and Greek quotations. Went to William and Mary College, studied law with an uncle, and was admitted to the bar at twenty. When his older brother died he inherited the family plantation but did not go to live there.

He was kind, modest, unassuming, and could easily be overlooked. He was more of a scholar than a courtroom lawyer. He was appointed to the first law professorship at William and Mary. Jefferson, John Marshall, and Henry Clay were his students.

He was poisoned by a grandnephew, George Wythe Sweeney, the leading beneficiary in his will. He signed the Declaration at fifty and died at eighty.

Francis Lightfoot Lee

FRANCIS LIGHTFOOT LEE, younger brother of Richard Henry, was a last-minute signer. He replaced Richard Bland, who had asked to be relieved because he was old and hurting.

Quiet and dignified, he did his best work in committees and in small groups. He did not remain in the federal government very long. Had no political ambitions. He quit Congress in 1779.

He served in Virginia's House of Burgesses and, unlike Richard Henry, he favored the adoption of the Constitution. He did his work in his brother's shadow. Francis was quiet, Richard outspoken. Contemporaries thought he was his brother's equal and in some regards superior.

In 1782, he decided to leave politics and went to live on his plantation called "Menokin" in Richmond County. He was forty-one when he signed, sixty-two when he died.

Carter Braxton

CARTER BRAXTON of Virginia could be called a reluctant signer. He succeeded Peyton Randolph, who had died. Virginians who were fearful of independence and democracy thought that in Braxton they had a man who would vote no. Listening to the debate and various points of view, he changed his mind.

He was the son of a wealthy plantation owner, attended William and Mary College. When his first wife died soon after marriage, he went to England for a time. Later, when the fires of independence were building, he was accused of having pro-British prejudice. However, as a member of Virginia's House of Burgesses, he soon swung to the side of the Patriots.

A member of Virginia's General Assembly for most of the rest of his life, he supported Jefferson's Bill for Religious Freedom.

His fortune was swallowed up in the war, leaving him bankrupt. He never did recover it and died in Richmond at the age of sixty-one.

Thos Nelson jr.

THOMAS NELSON of Virginia, described by John Adams: "a fat man...alert and lively for his weight."

Grandson of Thomas Nelson, wealthy merchant-planter who had come to America from Scotland, and son of William, president of the Council and acting governor of Virginia, young Thomas enjoyed the good things of life.

Educated at Cambridge in England, he returned to Virginia and was elected to the Council before he had gotten off the boat. He was twenty-six. His stay in England did not sway him from the idea of independence. He was Patriot all the way.

He resigned his commission as colonel in the militia to carry the Virginia resolution for independence all the way to Philadelphia.

During the war he urged General Washington to fire on his home, which was occupied by the British. In 1781 he was elected governor of Virginia. His health and his fortune were both damaged by the war. He died of asthma in 1789 at age fifty.

Joseph Hewes

JOSEPH HEWES, North Carolina, was born and bred in New Jersey as a Quaker. He slipped from the fold in adult life. Left Philadelphia in his early twenties for Edenton, North Carolina, where he became a successful merchant in the world of shipping.

An intense worker, he buried himself in whatever he had to do. A quiet man, he seldom spoke. As a member of the North Carolina Assembly he fought for colonial rights. However, it took him a while before he was convinced that a break with the mother country was the solution to the problem. Once convinced, he poured his energies into the task. John Adams considered his vote most important in bringing unanimity to the Congress.

During the war his shipping know-how was useful. He was virtually the first head of the U.S. Navy. He was responsible for getting John Paul Jones his first command of a U.S. Navy ship.

It is said that he died of overwork. Perhaps he died of a broken heart. His fiancée died before they were wed and he never married.

His signature is all business; not one extra stroke. Died in 1779 at the young age of forty-nine.

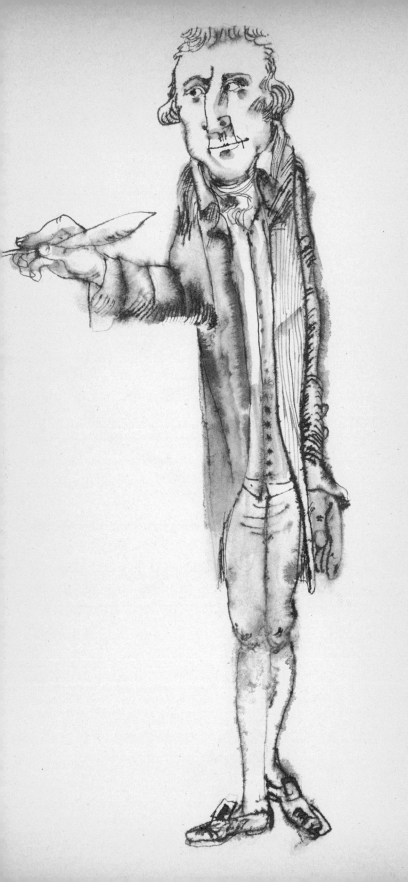

John Penn

JOHN PENN did not come from Pennsylvania. He was born in Virginia, went to a country school for a short time. He inherited his father's fortune and was able to devote himself to the study of the law in his rich uncle's library. So well did he learn that he was permitted to practice when he was twenty-one.

Moved to Williamsboro, North Carolina, where he opened an office. People liked him enough to elect him to the Continental Congress to support the patriotic cause.

A talkative man privately, he barely uttered a word in Congress. He joined with his two associates from North Carolina as they walked the path to independence. He had been deeply influenced by Thomas Paine's pamphlet *Common Sense.*

He retired from public life shortly after the war in poor health and died at the tender age of forty-eight.

Wm Hooper

WILLIAM HOOPER spoke rapidly and to the point. John Adams said he was a good orator. Born in Boston, son of a clergyman, law student of James Otis, he moved to North Carolina in his early twenties.

He practiced and lived in Wilmington. He was a deputy attorney general and was a member of Governor Tryon's militia. He was part of the expedition that subdued the western North Carolina frontiersmen who disliked the legislation from the east. They were called "Regulators"; embittered by their defeat, they favored the cause of the Loyalists.

Hooper was not present to vote on independence and didn't sign his name until late in the summer of 1776.

His popularity dimmed after the war. He was not reelected to Congress, probably because he favored adoption of the federal constitution.

He was the third of the North Carolina signers to die before reaching fifty. He passed away at age forty-eight.

ARTHUR MIDDLETON was born to a well-established, very wealthy South Carolina family. His father owned eight hundred slaves and had numerous plantations.

Arthur was educated in England and was an excellent Greek and Latin scholar. He was of medium stature, well-muscled, and hot of temper.

Despite his English education he was ruthless in his attitude and actions toward the Loyalists. The South Carolinians voted for the federation of the states against Britain. More important, however, was that the aristocracy of South Carolina had a good thing going for themselves and wanted to get away from British rule.

During the war Middleton was captured and imprisoned at Saint Augustine, along with Heyward and Rutledge, two other signers from South Carolina.

He was thirty-four when he signed, forty-four when he died.

Edward Rutledge J.

EDWARD RUTLEDGE was only twenty-six, the youngest to sign. He was of the landed gentry, dressed elegantly, and played the part of the aristocrat to the hilt.

His mother had her first baby when she was fifteen; her seventh was Edward, born when she was twenty-five. His father died when he was a year old.

His primary schooling took place in Charleston. Was sent to England, where he studied law at the Middle Temple; returned to Charleston in 1773, when he was twenty-three. As a member of the plantation aristocracy he entered public life very early. Elected to the Continental Congress, he was scorned by John Adams as a smart young peacock.

Nevertheless, when the chips were down, young Rutledge was most responsible for convincing the South Carolinians to vote for independence.

In 1798 he was elected governor of South Carolina and died two years later at age fifty.

Thomas Lynch Junr

THOMAS LYNCH, Jr., second youngest to sign at twenty-seven, was educated in England and studied law at the Middle Temple in London.

There were two Lynches from South Carolina at the Second Continental Congress, Thomas, Sr., and Thomas, Jr. The elder Lynch had suffered a severe stroke and had recovered sufficiently to try the trip to Philadelphia. His son had been elected with the idea of accompanying and caring for his father on the long trip north.

Lynch, Sr., was a wealthy rice planter, fiercely opposed to British rule. At Philadelphia he was so ill he was unable to attend the meeting. The son did and cast his vote for independence.

On the way home to South Carolina, the elder Lynch died in Annapolis, Maryland, and was buried there by his saddened son.

The health of Thomas, Jr., was not very good either. He had contracted malaria years earlier and did not have the strength to continue in public office. At age thirty he set sail with his wife for the West Indies, intending to continue to France, where Tom hoped to recover his health. They were never heard from again. Presumably their ship went down and they drowned.

Thos Heyward Junr

THOMAS HEYWARD, Jr., of South Carolina was only thirty when he signed. Born to a wealthy family on a huge plantation, he studied law at the Middle Temple in London and after five years was admitted to the bar. Began his practice when he was twenty-five.

He lived in England when the seeds for independence were germinating. When he returned to South Carolina he was thrust into public life and surprisingly became a Patriot.

He followed in the footsteps of his associate Arthur Middleton and did not go to Congress until the spring of 1776. His precise sentiments on independence in Philadelphia on July 2 are in question. The pressures for a unanimous declaration may have pushed him to vote yes.

When Charleston, South Carolina, fell he was captured by the British and held prisoner in Saint Augustine. He lived the longest of the South Carolina signers—to sixty-two.

Of all the signatures on the Declaration his is said to be the least legible.

Lyman Hall

LYMAN HALL brought his zeal for freedom to Georgia from Connecticut. Born in Wallingford, a graduate of Yale, he spent several years as an unsuccessful minister before becoming a physician.

He moved to Georgia to a new settlement of former New Englanders. It was Sunbury, in Saint John's Parish on the coast. He planted rice, continued his medical practice, and quickly found himself one of the leaders in this raw, sparsely populated community.

Georgia had no particular point of view concerning independence. The delegates went to Philadelphia with a free hand to vote as they saw fit.

Hall stayed in Congress until 1780; brought his family north to Wallingford, Connecticut, after the British destroyed his home.

He returned to Savannah, Georgia, and in 1783 was elected governor. While in office, he got the wheels rolling for what became Franklin College and the University of Georgia.

Signed at fifty-two, died at sixty-six.

Button Gwinnett

BUTTON GWINNETT, born in England of a Welsh family, came to America and settled in Savannah, Georgia, as a mature, married man. He was a merchant; purchased Saint Catherine's Island off the coast; planted it with rice, and prospered. Ten years before he signed the Declaration he showed little interest in public affairs. Lyman Hall spurred him on and before he knew it he had joined those who wanted independence.

Physically, he was a big man. He was polite, yet there was a fire in him that could explode at any time.

When he became chief executive of the state he found he had a strong difference with General Lachlan McIntosh about an unsuccessful expedition to Florida. McIntosh called Gwinnett a liar. A pistol duel took place; both men were wounded. The general recovered, Gwinnett died. He was forty-two.

His signature is the first one on the upper left of the document. Because he died so young and left so few signatures behind, some have been sold for as much as $14,000 at auction.

Geo Walton.

GEORGE WALTON was so small he appeared to be the youngest, but he was thirty-five. Edward Rutledge of South Carolina was only twenty-six.

Born in Virginia, orphaned as a boy, he was apprenticed by his uncle to a carpenter. Sensing his intelligence, the carpenter released him so that he could go to school. Mainly a self-taught man. He went to Savannah in 1769, studied law, and was admitted to the bar in 1774. Elected to the Continenal Congress, he accompanied Hall and Gwinnett to Philadelphia to vote for independence.

He was a British prisoner of war for nearly two years. He was released in 1779 and four years later helped draft a treaty with the Cherokee Indians. He helped in the development of the University of Georgia, was a judge in the state supreme court and later its chief justice.

As age crept up on him he appeared to grow more and more conservative. He lived until he was sixty-three.

ST. MARY'S COLLEGE OF MARYLAND LIBRARY
ST. MARY'S CITY, MARYLAND

C59571

E
221
.F55
1971   Fink, Sam
          The fifty-six who signed

059571 ✗

7 8

DATE DUE			